Nightmare
The Fright of Your Life

A horror thriller

Roger S. Moss

Samuel French — London
New York - Toronto - Hollywood

NIGHTMARE
THE FRIGHT OF YOUR LIFE

First presented at the Theatre Royal, Lincoln, on 5th
September 1992 by Michael Rose Ltd with the following
cast:

Miss Peterson/Jacqui Henderson	Jean Rogers
Jenny Gilman	Tracey Childs
Frank Gilman	David Kershaw
Mr Harvey/Mr Watson	Peter Byrne

Directed by Chris Moreno
Set designed by Alan Miller Bunford
Lighting by Graham McLusky
Sound designed by Clement Rawling
Original Music by Malcolm Newton

CHARACTERS

Miss Peterson
Jenny Gilman
Frank Gilman
Mr Harvey
Mr Watson
Jacqui Henderson

NB The parts of Miss Peterson and Jacqui Henderson are played by the same actress, and those of Mr Watson and Mr Harvey by the same actor. This fact should be disguised in any publicity for the play

The action of the play takes place in an apartment in a converted chapel

ACT I	Scene 1	Late afternoon in October
	Scene 2	Three weeks later
	Scene 3	A few minutes later
ACT II	Scene 1	The following morning
	Scene 2	Sunday, late afternoon
	Scene 3	Later that night

Time — the present

My grateful thanks to
C.D.M.

ACT I

Scene 1

The living-room and bedroom of an apartment in a converted chapel. October. Late afternoon

At the rear of the room is an open staircase, modern in design, leading to an open-plan bedroom, in which a double bed, bedside table and dressing table can be seen. A door leads off from L of the bedroom to an unseen bathroom and dressing-room. R of the staircase are two doors, one a cupboard door and the other, with a small, square, frosted-glass window in it, leading to the unseen cellar and kitchen. Beyond these is a large stained-glass window surrounded by stonework; this is the last remaining sign of the chapel's original splendour. There is a grand fireplace R of this window with fire irons beside it. L of the staircase are french windows bordered by grand-looking curtains; even further L is the front door. Among the furnishings, which can be at the designer's discretion, there are a drinks cabinet, a sofa with a coffee table in front of it, on which are magazines, newspapers, paper and pens, and a side table with a lamp and telephone on it

As the House Lights fade, dramatic music begins. In the darkness, the Curtain *rises. The Lights come up slowly to reveal clothes and books in evidence in the room, making it plain that someone is living in the apartment. The curtains over the french windows are closed. The stained-glass window glows with a strange light. The Light outside the window suggests that the sun is slowly sinking*

The front door opens abruptly. The music stops. After a momentary struggle with the door, Miss Peterson enters, followed closely by Frank Gilman and his fiancée Jenny

Miss Peterson I'm sorry, the door is rather stiff but solid, very solid. I've been meaning to have the door fixed for some time. However, I must make sure Mr Harvey has a note of it. That's the beauty of these conversions, you get the best of both worlds. Now let's see if I can throw some light on this situation. (*She opens the curtains over the french windows; light floods in*)

Jenny Oh, it's a beautiful home. Frank, isn't it a beautiful home? It's got such atmosphere, yes, real atmosphere; you can almost feel it, don't you think so, Frank? (*She indicates the stained-glass window*) Oh, and that window, it is just divine. What do you think? Frank, say something!

Frank It looks expensive to me. How much is the rent per month, Miss Peterson?

Miss Peterson Very reasonable, Mr Gilman, for this area. It works out to around eight hundred a month.

Frank Jenny, that's not exactly cheap.

Miss Peterson But don't forget it comes complete with your own housemaid who services this and next door on a daily basis. Although I must say it doesn't look like she's been in as yet. Now, Mrs Gilman, what more could a newly-wed want?

Jenny Well, Miss Peterson, we don't actually get married till next month. So please call me Jenny.

Frank exits through the french windows to the outside

Miss Peterson Oh, I'm sorry, I thought you were already — well, never mind. Come on, let me show you around. As you can see it is an unusual property. It is just about to come back on the market. The present occupant will be leaving in a few weeks' time. He's going to move on to bigger and better things. I'm so sorry about the mess but he didn't know you were coming round today. We couldn't get hold of him before he left for work. We had to ring him there so he apologizes. The chapel itself was converted some twelve years ago but before that had remained empty for twenty years. It was built in the late seventeen-hundreds.

Frank enters

Frank So who is buried in that old graveyard next door?

Miss Peterson Most of those graves date back to that time. It hasn't been used for years and years although it is still maintained by Mr Harvey; he's the gardener for both this property and the one next door. Nowadays the locals use the church on the other side of the village.

Frank Well, that's comforting to know. At least we won't have to see the local dead being buried whilst eating Sunday lunch!

Jenny Frank, don't be so morbid. I am sorry, Miss Peterson. You'll have to forgive my fiancé's sense of humour.

Miss Peterson That's quite all right. We have tried to get the graves relocated but I am afraid there is a protection order of some sort. But as you saw it is well maintained by the groundsman. It's really rather quaint.

Frank Is that what it means when it says, "Close to all local amenities"? Who would have thought all these conveniences could be so handy!

Jenny Frank, you are the limit sometimes.

Frank Only trying to be positive.

Miss Peterson The stained-glass window dates right back to the eighteenth century, although most of the glass has now been replaced I believe. However it is a most attractive feature. The conversion was done by Jordans in London and I must say they did an extremely good job. We never have any problems letting this property each time it comes on the market.

Frank Does it come on the market often, then?

Miss Peterson No, I wouldn't say often, but people do tend to come and go these days.

Jenny (opening the cupboard door; the cupboard is empty) Is this a bathroom downstairs?

Miss Peterson No. That is a cupboard for your domestic appliances. The bathroom is upstairs. There is a dressing-room next to the bedroom and the bathroom leads off from that. It is a well-thought-out design using space in a very modern way. When would you require the property?

Jenny wanders upstairs into the bedroom

Frank As soon as it's available, but we have got other properties to consider.

Jenny (from the upper level) But Frank, we haven't seen anything quite like this. The village looked lovely as we drove through and it's only a couple of miles from the motorway. You can be in the city in less than an hour.

Miss Peterson That is the beauty of this particular location. It is quiet but not too isolated because you know civilization is never too far away. We have always found that to be an excellent incentive to most of our clients.

Frank Yes, your colleague Mr Watson said we should look at this straight away. Are you the only agents in the village?

Miss Peterson In such a small village there would be insufficient trade to keep us alive if we had competitors.

Frank It's dog-eat-dog in your business, I guess.

Miss Peterson So to speak!

Jenny (*coming back down the stairs into the living-room*) Honey, look at
that bedroom.
Peterson Very open plan.
Frank Maybe we could sell tickets — nightly performances!
Jenny Miss Peterson, could you tell me where the kitchen is?
Miss Peterson Oh, you'll not need to know where that is very often, not
if I know Mrs Gregory. Mrs Gregory — she's the housemaid — she'll
do your shopping, cleaning, washing up, and even a spot of cooking. The
door leads down to the cellar kitchen, fully fitted with all you'll ever
need.

*Jenny exits to the kitchen. Frank climbs the stairs, looks round the
bedroom and then looks off into the dressing-room*

Miss Peterson That's the dressing-room and bathroom.
Frank Yes. Thank you.

Jenny screams, off. Frank runs down the stairs

Jenny enters from the kitchen

Jenny Frank, oh, you'll never guess.
Frank What is it? What's down there?
Jenny There's the most beautiful Aga cooker. Oh, I've always wanted to
have an Aga.
Frank And I've always wanted a heart attack. Jenny, you frightened the
life out of me.
Miss Peterson Jenny, come and see the bathroom.
Frank Please God, if she sees it's got a bidet she may give birth!
Jenny Take no notice, Miss Peterson. Frank, that's how rumours start, and
we don't want the village gossiping.

*The shadowy figure of Mr Harvey, the gardener, appears at the french
windows, looking in*

My God, who's that?
Miss Peterson Oh, it's only Mr Harvey, I expect; the gardener I was
telling you about. Come in, Mr Harvey. (*She moves to open the
windows*)

Mr Harvey moves away before Miss Peterson can open the windows

Miss Peterson Mr Harvey, Mr Harvey! Where did he go? He is rather set in his own ways and I suspect rather shy of new tenants.

Frank Presuming we become the new tenants.

Miss Peterson Listen, I have to check the outside of the building so perhaps you would like a few minutes by yourselves to discuss the situation. I won't be too long.

Miss Peterson exits through the french windows

Jenny Frank, why are you being so obstructive? You know we haven't seen anything that we both like.

Frank Jen, we still haven't. It's not particularly cheap and it's rather strange to have the bedroom at the top of your lounge!

Jenny I think it's a lovely conversion. There's plenty of space for the two of us. Oh, please, Frank.

Frank Well, why don't we spend some more time looking around before we decide. You know we don't have to say yes here and now.

Jenny Frank, we have seen nearly a dozen properties and none of them are anywhere near as nice as this. I don't understand you sometimes. We've spent weeks trudging around looking at homes, some of which were so awful we virtually ran out and now we've found this marvellous home, and you want to think about it!

Frank Listen, Jen. I'm not trying to be awkward, it's just I want things to be right for us in our first home, that's all.

Jenny I know. I want them to be right too. The thing is, if we don't get sorted out soon, when we come back from our honeymoon you won't be able to carry me over the threshold because there won't be one.

Frank OK. OK. You're right, I guess. Let's weigh up the pros and cons. This place is big enough. It has a bedroom with dressing-room and bathroom *en suite*. It's furnished so we can move straight in.

Jenny The kitchen is fully fitted and comes with a housekeeper.

Frank You're not trying to avoid your marital vows are you?

Jenny There's nothing in there about "to slave and to sweat".

Frank But I do recall something about "to have and to hold".

Frank grabs Jenny and pulls her into an embrace. They kiss

Jenny Frank, you're changing the subject. Besides, Miss Peterson might return.

Frank Sorry, it doesn't have a spare bedroom.

Jenny That's only a small con.

Frank No, it's definitely a pro; it means your mother can't come and stay. In fact, now I think about it, this isn't such a bad place at all.

Jenny You can be such a sod sometimes. Anyway, leaving the fact my mother cannot stay, are we agreed that we'll take it here and now?

Frank Yes, boss, we'll take it.

Miss Peterson enters through the french windows

Miss Peterson Everything seems to be in order on the outside. It's one of the benefits of these old buildings: very solid. Have you decided what you would care to do?

Frank Yes. Suddenly it seems a very attractive idea. We would like to move in after our honeymoon. That's three weeks this weekend.

Miss Peterson That'll be fine. I will get Mr Watson to send you the papers if you let me have your address and bank details.

During the following, Frank writes down the information necessary for the purchase of the house on a piece of paper from the coffee table

He'll get a standing order form for you to fill in. We can send the keys on as well if that's more convenient. I'm sure you will be very happy.

Jenny Thank you for your time, Miss Peterson. I think it is just perfect.

Miss Peterson We've never had any complaints so far.

Jenny Well that is settled, Frank. At least you've got a threshold to carry me over when we get back from honeymoon.

Miss Peterson Are you going somewhere exotic?

Frank It should be for the money it's costing.

Jenny It's somewhere in the Caribbean. Frank won't tell me where. In fact he wouldn't have told me at all if it wasn't for the fact we had to go for our inoculations yesterday.

Frank (*indicating his paper*) Do you want me to drop these details in with Mr Watson?

Miss Peterson No! I'll take it now. Mr Watson is out with another client at the moment.

Frank (*handing Miss Peterson the paper*) OK. There you are. Look forward to hearing from you. (*To Jenny*) We return on ... ?

Jenny Saturday the fourteenth.

Frank Can we move straight in?

Miss Peterson Saturday the fourteenth; that's fine. It will give the housekeeper enough time to do a good spring clean before your arrival.
Jenny Thank you again, Miss Peterson.
Miss Peterson My pleasure.

Frank moves to the front door and again has difficulty opening it

I'm so sorry. Let me help. (*She helps Frank to open the door*)
Jenny Goodbye.
Frank Goodbye.
Miss Peterson Happy honeymoon. Good luck with the wedding.

Frank and Jenny exit

Miss Peterson watches them go, then looks at the sheet of paper handed her by Frank. After a pause she walks over to the drinks cabinet and pours herself a glass of scotch

Mr Harvey appears behind the french windows

(*Without looking at Mr Harvey*) Well, you were not very friendly, *Mr Harvey*. I hope you will not be so shy when Mr and Mrs Gilman settle in after they're married. (*She takes a packet of cigarettes from her bag and lights one. She moves over to the fireplace and stands with her back to it, looking inwards to the room*) It's no good starting them off in a nervous state of mind or we'll frighten them off. I think these two will do very nicely. Take this. (*She hands him the paper with the address on it*) You've got some preparation to do. Locate the records. That's the present address, which should help. We're going to have to move fast on this one. However, we've got three weeks to make sure everything is in place. That should just give us sufficient time to get the last shipment away. We must make that flight date. Yes, I think these two will do very nicely — to have and to hold from this day forth ——
Mr Harvey — till death us do part!

Black-out

CURTAIN

The theme music plays

Scene 2

The same. Three weeks later

As the music fades, the Curtain *rises. The room is now tidy. The curtains are open and light is flooding through the windows. This slowly fades to darkness as the scene proceeds. A torch has been set under the coffee table*

There is the sound of banging from outside the front door; the door flies open and Frank enters, carrying Jenny in his arms

Frank Well, Mrs Gilman, welcome home. God, you've put on weight. It was all that lobster you had — not to mention the wine. (*He lays Jenny full length on the sofa*)
Jenny You're a fine one to talk. I had to carry you to the bridal suite several times in the last couple of weeks so don't come the hard-done-by husband with me!
Frank Now don't move a muscle. I'll get the rest of the bags. I've brought the biggest one in first.

Jenny throws a cushion at Frank. He ducks. He then collects other suitcases from outside the front door, bringing them into the lounge. Among the cases is a duty -free bag with a bottle of whisky in it

Jenny I think this is what they call married bliss.
Frank You've had a very exhausting honeymoon. You take it easy, I can manage! (*He switches on the lights, closes the front door and leans against it*) Well, Mrs Gilman, we're together again, for better or worse, richer or poorer.
Jenny I don't recall anything about being poor a part of our marriage vows. You either keep me in the style to which I want to become accustomed or it's instant divorce.
Frank (*climbing on top of Jenny*) You're not fickle, are you? And there was me thinking it was only my body you were after.

They kiss passionately

There is a rumble of distant thunder; the Light outside the windows begins to dim more quickly, as if a storm is approaching

Jenny I know you're keen to christen this sofa but we've got some unpacking to do.

Jenny gets up, throwing Frank to the floor. They collect the cases. Jenny switches on the upstairs lights from the light switch downstairs, but in doing so switches off the lights downstairs. She corrects her mistake and they carry the cases up the stairs, depositing them in the dressing-room, off, then returning to the bedroom. They sit on the bed

Frank The estate agent says he would call round when we returned to sign some papers that weren't through before we left.
Jenny I thought we'd signed everything before we left for the Caribbean. Surely there can't be more paperwork?
Frank John Watson, that's the other partner, rang before we left to say he'd stop round with the remaining forms. The standing orders must be signed along with insurance documents and a copy of our contract for this place. I saw no harm in getting them out of the way before we get settled here. Look, I'm going to have a shower. Perhaps you would like to get me a glass of something long, cool and refreshing.

Jenny slowly removes Frank's jacket and unbuttons his shirt, then begins to remove his trousers

Jenny Certainly, sir, what's your pleasure? A cocktail? Harvey Wall-banger, Screwdriver, Between the Sheets ——

The phone rings

(*Jumping up*) I'll get it! (*She runs downstairs and picks up the receiver*)
Frank Well, it doesn't look as if I'm going to!

Frank exits into the dressing-room

Jenny (*into the phone*) Hallo ... um ... Six-o-seven-three. Hallo ... hallo. (*She puts the receiver down*)

There is a rumble of thunder, louder than the one before. Jenny moves to the french windows and looks out. The phone rings again. Jenny dashes to the phone and picks up the receiver

(*Into the phone*) Six-o-seven-three. Hallo. ... Oh, hallo. ... Yes, we've just got back. ... Well, thank you, Mum, but we should be OK. ... I promise. ... Yes, we did get the earlier flight. ... I'm glad we did ... at least we've got the whole weekend to get it sorted. ... No, we'll manage. Frank is determined to get it done on his own. ... I'm sure he will. Mum, did you ring earlier?... Oh, well, it must have been a wrong number. ... No. ... There seemed to be someone at the other end but they just listened. ... As I say, probably just a wrong number. ... All right, I'll speak to you later. ... Bye. (*She puts the receiver down, looks around and then dashes back up the stairs*) Frank, we must get an extension put up here. We can't leap downstairs every time the phone rings.

Frank (*off*) Who was that?

Jenny Mother.

Frank (*off*) What did she want?

Jenny She wanted to know if we were able to get the earlier flight and to ask if we needed any help this weekend.

Frank (*off*) I hope you put her off. That's all we need: the Spanish Inquisition into our honeymoon! Who was the other call?

Jenny I don't know. I think it was a wrong number because they rang off more or less straight away. I wish people wouldn't do that. I think it's so rude.

Frank (*off*) Not many people have this number yet, do they?

Jenny Only Mother and your office. I must get some cards out to let people know we're here.

Frank (*off*) I've just had a thought. You don't think she's just going to turn up out of the blue and surprise us?

Jenny No. Mum would never do that. Anyway she knows she can't stay here. You made that obvious at the reception.

Frank (*off*) I was only winding her up. I didn't mean to gloat. She knows I always joke with her.

Jenny Yes, I don't think even she believed we could only be reached by helicopter!

Frank (*off*) I told her she could visit for the day — if she had to!

Frank enters from the dressing-room, dripping wet and wearing nothing but a towel

Jenny You are so obvious, Frank. I can read you like a book.

Frank Good! Then we can bypass the introduction and go straight to chapter one.

Jenny Will you take a hold of yourself?

Frank I'd much rather take a hold of you.

Jenny Frank, you're soaking wet. Will you please go and dry off. Second thoughts, go back into the shower and turn on the cold.

Frank What happened to the romance of our honeymoon? Sun-soaked beaches. Cocktails by the pool. Dancing till dawn. You've soon turned into a housewife.

Jenny No, I haven't. It is just one of us should stay vertical for at least ten minutes so we can get unpacked and sorted out. You're back at work on Monday and there are tons of things to do. God, I wish we were still away. (*She gestures to the window*) We left to avoid this weather and look what we've returned to.

Frank Anyway, like what? What things?

Jenny Well, like … come on, Frank, you've got to remember I'm new at this. Well, like all the washing and ironing has to be done. There's shopping to do, we must collect the rest of our stuff from Mum and a whole lot of things I want to spend your money on. The first thing is to do this place the way we want it.

Frank Jen, slow down. I'll help. I'll show you where the washing machine is and then you can get started. I'll give you the car keys so you can go shopping and I'll give you your own bank account because I've gone right off the idea of a joint one.

Jenny If I thought for one moment you were serious!

Frank Yes — and what would you do?

Jenny Well, for one thing, you could forget about prancing around trying to turn me on because I am sure, with all that washing and ironing, shopping and worrying about my finances I would have the most enormous thumping great headache!

Jenny pushes Frank on to the bed; he grabs her and pulls her down with him. They both laugh

There is a loud clap of thunder

Jenny Pack it in. (*She laughs*) Frank, it doesn't work!

Frank I'm sorry, Jen. You're absolutely right. Would you do me a favour though?

Jenny What's that?

Frank When you go shopping, would you get a big bottle of aspirin!

Jenny (*hitting Frank playfully*) You sod, you're just a male chauvinist pig!

*They embrace on the bed for some time. There are a huge flash of lightning
and clap of thunder. The Lights go out leaving the stage in semi-darkness*

Jenny Frank ...
Frank What the hell was that? Listen ...
Jenny The storm must be above us. Do you know where the fuse box is?
Frank You've just been fighting for equality — why don't you go and find
out?
Jenny Frank, please go. You know I hate storms. Try the cupboard under
the stairs.

*Frank slowly gets off the bed and makes his way carefully downstairs. He
moves to the windows to pull back the curtains. He then goes to the
cupboard door and tries to open it*

Frank Bloody thing's locked. (*He heads towards the kitchen door*)

*The kitchen door swings open and Miss Peterson enters, carrying a
torch pointed upwards at her face*

A clap of thunder sounds; Frank, Jenny and Miss Peterson all scream

Frank Miss Peterson! What the hell are you doing here?
Miss Peterson I might ask you the same question. You gave me such a
fright, standing there with nothing on. We weren't expecting you back
until tomorrow. You shouldn't be here — I mean I'm not ready for you.
I've still got a lot of preparation to do. Does Mr Watson know you're
back because if he does, he should have told me!
Frank No he doesn't. We've come a day early but never mind that —
where the hell is the fuse box?

The Lights flicker back on

Miss Peterson I expect it was another power cut. We quite often get them
during a storm. Look, I think I should ring Mr Watson, if you don't mind.
(*She moves to the telephone and begins to dial a number*)
Jenny I am so sorry, Miss Peterson. It's just we didn't think anyone would
mind as you said the place would be clear by the weekend.
Miss Peterson Well, no, that's right, but there is still a great deal of
cleaning to be done and I was just checking to see if Mrs Gregory had

completed before your return tomorrow.

Jenny Do these cuts happen regularly?

Miss Peterson Usually when we have a storm. Being a bit isolated the supply to the house is pretty old. However we always get back on very soon because of the priority to the airport. I think the village is lucky in that respect. (*She listens to the phone*) Damn, I've got the machine. (*She hangs up*)

Jenny I didn't realize we were near an airport.

Miss Peterson You're not, strictly speaking. It's the RAF station about twenty miles down the road. You sometimes see the pilots in the local pub.

Frank I'm afraid we haven't — not yet, anyway.

Miss Peterson What made you return early? You gave me such a shock.

Jenny We got an earlier flight back which meant we didn't have to travel overnight arriving at six in the morning.

Frank The weather was poor the last couple of days so we saw no point in hanging around much longer so I was able to transfer our flights.

Miss Peterson I see. There's no real problem. It's just that I was thrown a little. We've lost a day now and I'm trying to think what else there is to do.

Jenny Don't worry, Miss Peterson, we can do the rest. Besides, everything looks done.

Miss Peterson No! I mean, I'll be able to sort it out.

Frank It's no trouble. Jenny's got some washing she wants to do so she'll be in the kitchen anyway.

Jenny Come on, Miss Peterson, I'll give you a hand. (*She heads towards the cellar door*)

Miss Peterson Well, I'd appreciate it if you would leave me alone down there so I can finish off checking the inventory. I'll have to complete the rest next week. Then I'll get out of your way so you can do what you have to do.

Jenny Don't be silly. We'll soon make light work of it if there are two pairs of hands. (*She heads for the cellar door again*)

There is a knock at the front door and a distant rumble of thunder

Miss Peterson I'll answer the door. After all, we don't want to frighten anyone away. (*She opens the door*)

John Watson is revealed in the doorway. He is very smartly dressed in

*a suit, with an overcoat in one hand and a briefcase in the other. He does
not see Frank or Jenny*

Mr Watson What the hell is that car doing outside?
Miss Peterson Do come in, sir. (*Warningly*) The Gilmans have arrived a
   day early.

Mr Watson steps into the room and sees Frank in his state of undress

Mr Watson Right ... I thought you were arriving tomorrow. I didn't
   realize you were back already. I was wondering who had parked their
   car in your drive.
Frank Don't worry, it's ours. I'm sorry ... (*He indicates Jenny*) My wife,
   Jenny. (*To Jenny*) Mr Watson.
Mr Watson How considerate! How nice to meet you, Mrs Gilman.
Jenny Thank you. Frank, go upstairs and get dressed. We've only just
   arrived back and Frank was just having a shower when he bumped into
   Miss Peterson. Not in the shower.
Miss Peterson Listen, before you completely destroy my reputation in the
   village I'll quickly finish off down in the kitchen, while Mr Watson sorts
   things out up here.

*Frank goes upstairs and exits to the dressing-room; Miss Peterson exits
to the cellar kitchen*

Mr Watson I am so sorry, I have obviously caught you at a bad moment.
   We didn't get a chance to meet before you were married. I was going to
   call round on Monday. I have some papers for your husband to sign. I
   may as well get it done now, seeing you're here. As I said, I'm sorry if
   it's inconvenient.
Jenny Please don't apologize. We got an earlier flight but I'm afraid
   we've caught Miss Peterson unawares. She seems very efficient. I'm
   sorry we have very little in yet, but I can offer you a duty-free scotch.
Mr Watson A scotch would be fine, thank you.
Jenny Now all I need to do is find some glasses. (*She starts to search*)
Mr Watson (*indicating the drinks cabinet*) I think you'll find the glasses
   in that cabinet.
Jenny Oh, thank you. (*She fetches two glasses from the cabinet and sets
   about pouring the whisky*)
Mr Watson Did you have a good honeymoon?

Jenny Yes, thank you. Such a shame the weather changed for the worse in the last couple of days, but, looking on the bright side, at least we have the full weekend to get settled before we rejoin the rat race.

Mr Watson So you're here tonight?

Jenny Oh, yes, that's one of the reasons we came back early. That is all right, isn't it? I mean, I know our contract doesn't begin until tomorrow but as nobody is here and quite honestly it's too late to go anywhere else …

Mr Watson No, no, that's fine. There's no problem.

Miss Peterson enters with her coat and bag

Jenny Miss Peterson, would you like a drink?

Miss Peterson I'd love a whisky.

Jenny fetches another glass and pours Miss Peterson a whisky

Mr Watson Could I have a little water with mine?

Jenny Of course.

Miss Peterson I'll get it.

Jenny Don't go down again. Stay here, I'll go.

Jenny exits to the cellar kitchen

Mr Watson gets his papers out of his briefcase and carefully places them together on the table

The musical underscore begins

Miss Peterson Looks like we're in for a storm this weekend.

Mr Watson What the hell are they doing here? This is turning into a mess already. How the hell do I get rid of it with these two *in situ* ? They're not stupid, you know. One hint of anything odd, one loose word from either of us and they'll be out of here and down to the police before we even know what's happened.

Miss Peterson I know, I'm as concerned as you are. I've managed to clear the kitchen so it's just your "problem" that remains to be got rid of. Somehow, some way, it must be done this weekend. In the meantime it is under lock and key.

Mr Watson Good. Then we must get them to leave the house for a couple of hours then we can finish off. In the meantime both of their files have been cleared. I've just got to get them to sign these papers and I heard today that our clients have now confirmed shipment.

Miss Peterson That's a relief. When is it?

Mr Watson Monday night. That's another reason I didn't want any further problems here. I suppose if the worse comes to the worst, we could let these two go. It means giving up at least one hundred thousand pounds. Bugger it! Why did they have to get here early?

There is a distant roll of thunder and the underscore stops

Jenny enters with a jug of water

Jenny There we go. Say when. (*She pours water into Mr Watson's glass*)

Mr Watson When. Thank you.

Miss Peterson downs her drink in one, picks up her bag and makes for the door

Miss Peterson Well, I must be going. I've got a lot to do this weekend. You'll find everything you need downstairs. Thank you for the drink Mrs Gilman. Good-night, John. I'll see you tomorrow.

Miss Peterson exits

Frank enters from the dressing-room and comes down the stairs

Frank Good-night Miss Peterson! (*To the others*) Do you think I've frightened her off? Sorry to keep you waiting, Mr Watson. Now what are these papers I hear I need to look at?

Mr Watson Nothing to look at, just the standing order, the insurance on this place and I've got your copy of the lease. I checked them through earlier to save you time. I don't want to intrude, especially on your first day back from honeymoon. It just requires your signatures where I have crossed. You, too, Mrs Gilman, if you don't mind.

Jenny (*signing*)That's that. Darling, would you like to join us for a drink to celebrate the fact we have probably signed our lives away.

Mr Watson chokes on his drink

Frank Are you OK, Mr Watson?

Mr Watson Oh, yes, I am fine, I guess it just went down the wrong way. Please, I'm just fine now. Well, I really must not take up any more of your time. Thank you so much for the drink and for signing these last few bits and pieces. I'll get copies of these sent round. I really ought to go before this storm gets any worse. I do hope it doesn't rain all weekend. I was going to play golf but it looks like I may have to abandon that idea.

Jenny Oh, by the way, have you a key to that cupboard?

Mr Watson That cupboard? Oh, I'm sure we have it somewhere. I'll see what I can find and have it sent round to you.

Jenny And don't forget.

Mr Watson Forget what?

Jenny The key.

Mr Watson Oh, yes, the key. I won't forget, indeed I can't forget! Good-night to you both.

Frank and Jenny show Mr Watson over to the door and he quickly exits with his briefcase and coat

Frank (*referring to the whisky glasses*) I'll get rid of these downstairs.

Frank picks up the glasses and exits to the kitchen. Jenny goes to the window, then turns and switches on more lights

The telephone rings. Jenny picks up the receiver

Jenny Hallo, six–o–seven–three. ... Why hallo. ...Yes, we've only just arrived back. ... Jenny ... Jenny Gilman. How nice of you to call ... that's very neighbourly of you, Jacqui. ... We'd love to but we haven't finished unpacking. ... Well, why don't you pop round here and join Frank and I. We can christen our new home ... No, really, we'd love to meet you. OK. Well, maybe later. Thanks again ... Bye. (*She hangs up*)

The Lights flicker and go out, then immediately come back on. Frank yells, off. Jenny runs to the cellar door

Jenny Frank, are you all right? Frank! Frank!

Frank enters from the cellar

Frank I'm fine. Tripped up the steps when the lights went out.

Jenny Sure you're OK?

Frank Fine. Who was on the phone?

Jenny Jacqui Henderson. She's our next-door-neighbour apparently. She invited us round for a drink but I've persuaded her to come round here instead.

Frank That's great. Come round here ... we've got nothing to offer. I had better go and get stocked up.

Jenny I'll come with you, then.

Frank Tell you what, why don't you get some food together while I'm out. I won't be long, I promise.

Jenny Well, take an umbrella, otherwise you'll get soaked.

Frank I've got that golf umbrella in the back of the car, I'll use that. I'll be back soon.

They kiss

Frank exits

Jenny moves to close the curtains over the french windows. Before she can do so, all the Lights go out inside the chapel

Jenny Oh shit, that's all I need.

She moves to find the torch, which is placed under the table, turning her back to the french windows as she does so

A shadowy figure — Jacqui Henderson, in fact, with a black coat pulled up over her head — appears outside the french windows

The underscore begins

Jenny picks up the torch, turns round and the shadowy figure disappears. Jenny closes the curtains. She moves to the telephone with the torch and picks up the receiver. She is about to dial when the cellar door slams shut. She carefully replaces the receiver

Hallo, is somebody there? Hallo ...

She moves toward the cellar, opens the door slowly and shines the torch inside. The french windows bang, lightning flashes and thunder rumbles.

Jenny screams, quickly shutting the cellar door. She puts down the torch, moves slowly over to the curtains and draws them back in one swift movement. There is nothing to see. Jenny quickly shuts the doors and locks them and returns to the telephone, dials and listens

Please answer, please, please.

She slowly turns round. There begins a series of thuds at the front door. Jenny hangs up the telephone, picks up the poker from the fireplace and then heads for the door. She stands by the door, the poker raised above her head.

The door bursts open. Jenny screams loudly

The underscore plays

Black-out

CURTAIN

SCENE 3

The same. A few minutes later

The door is now shut and a black raincoat is hanging from the side of a chair

The CURTAIN *rises on Jenny outstretched on the couch and Jacqui Henderson standing by the drinks cabinet, pouring brandy*

Jacqui Darling, I thought you were a goner for certain. Here, drink this brandy. I've no idea if it will do you good but I always feel better with alcohol inside me. Oh, I'm so sorry, we haven't properly been introduced. We spoke on the telephone earlier. Jacqui, Jacqui Henderson, from next door. (*She hands the brandy to Jenny*) I never thought when you said "Come round for a drink" I'd end up being nurse for the night.
Jenny I am so sorry, but what happened? All I can remember is the door, someone thumping at the door and then this horrific shape, this *thing*.

Jacqui Well, darling, I've been called some things in my time but I've never given anyone the fright of their lives. Listen, Jenny, I was outside for at least five minutes trying to get in. We had a power cut; we're always having them round here. The least excuse and the electricity board cut this village off. I think they do it deliberately nowadays: "Ooh, who shall we cause havoc with tonight? ... Oh, I know, let's turn off the lights in Milbury again."

Jenny But did you not see anything at the door?

Jacqui Darling, the lights were out in the village. I don't carry a flashlight with me when I go next door for drinks; it usually is a bottle of something or other, and tonight it was brandy which is just as well, I think, in the circumstances.

Jenny Jacqui, I felt so frightened. You must have seen something. This thing was such an odd shape.

Jacqui Darling, I didn't want to frighten you, but perhaps it would be better if you both stayed somewhere else for the weekend, until the police sort things out.

Jenny So there was someone!

Jacqui I didn't say that. But I have heard there have been a couple of burglaries in the village and if you are nervous it may be best for you and Frank to leave until they catch whoever it is. I could always let you know how progress is going.

Jenny No! This is our first home together. I'll be damned if I'll be made to leave by some bastard intent on robbing us. It's over now. Maybe there wasn't anyone anyway. I was just jet-lagged. My imagination was playing tricks.

They both laugh. Jenny gets up off the couch and pours herself another drink

I feel better now. Thank you so much, I feel very embarrassed. What a way to begin. You see, Frank and I only just ... my goodness, where's Frank? He only went to the off-licence. How long was I out for, Jacqui?

Jacqui Oh, I'd say at least ... two minutes. Listen, Jenny, don't worry. I saw your husband leave not fifteen minutes ago. By the time he finds the off-licence and gets served it will be another five minutes before he gets back. The trouble is, in this place, everything is so slow. Nobody rushes anywhere to do anything in this village. Old Stan will have young Frank chatting for ages. That's the beauty, everything goes at a different pace. Although I must say I prefer the city sometimes if only to get a bit of excitement back into life.

Jenny How long have you lived here?

Jacqui I'd say about twelve years. I moved down here when my husband disappeared.

Jenny Oh, I'm sorry.

Jacqui Yes, he only went out to the off-licence; I never saw him again!

Jenny What?

Jacqui Oh, darling don't be so gullible. The little shit left me. We got divorced years ago. Best thing really. He couldn't keep up with me — different tastes, let's say — I had taste and he didn't. Best thing really for both of us, especially for me. He screwed around and I screwed a fortune out of him in settlement, then I moved down here for a change of scene. It does you good to change your habits every so often.

Jenny Do you have children?

Jacqui Only when there aren't any men around! (*She laughs*) Thank the Lord we did not have any little offspring. Could you imagine me with kids? Oh, the very thought makes me shudder. It would only remind me of him, which would be like having permanent indigestion, a life-long reminder of what you'd had the night before.

Jenny Frank and I want to have a family.

Jacqui Darling, do forgive me. Here I am ranting and raving like some embittered old hag about the downfall of marriage and here are you having just returned from honeymoon. How very insensitive of me. You and Frank will be fine, I'm sure. Just check his collar for lipstick and his jacket for hair when he comes in. You never know.

Jenny I think Frank will be pushing his luck to wander from the path so early.

Jacqui Darling, men were born to wander. From an early age their eyes wander, followed closely by their hands. Then their legs catch on and you never see them for dust.

Jenny Have you seen your husband since you broke up?

Jacqui No, thank God! The son-of-a-bitch wouldn't dare show his face round here for fear of having his balls sautéed in oil.

Jenny That's a bit extreme.

Jacqui That's just for starters. Hey, listen, let's not talk about my downfalls, let's talk about you two. What does he do, this fella of yours? Is he rich? Is he good in the sack and does he have any disgusting habits you wish to discuss?

Jenny Well, yes, yes and no — well, none that I'm aware of.

Jacqui Yet! That's the trouble with men. They go off after a while and you discover those little holes in their characters you never saw before, when you were blinded by love. They slurp over you like a bowl of soup when you're fresh and hot and then move on to the next course before you get a chance to cool off.

Jenny Well, I intend to make a meal of our marriage rather than just have a starter.

Frank enters with a bottle of champagne wrapped in paper and a golf umbrella

Frank Hi, Jenny. I'm so sorry I've been gone so long.

Jacqui This must be cock-a-leekie.

Jenny Frank, this is Jacqui Henderson, our next door neighbour. She just popped in for a drink and found me on the floor.

Frank Why?

Jacqui I gave Jenny a bit of a scare.

Frank and Jacqui shake hands; during the following Frank unwraps the bottle

Frank Well, Jacqui, perhaps you'd like to join us in a glass of the bubbly? What happened then, Jenny? Are you all right?

Jenny I'm fine now, thanks to Jacqui.

Jacqui That's very kind of you, Frank. I'd better be careful, though; I've already had some of the brandy I brought for your housewarming.

Frank That's very good of you. Jenny, some for you?

Jenny Actually, no Frank, none for me, if you don't mind. It's just that I don't feel all that comfortable. I guess I'll be all right. I think I should have something to eat. Jacqui, would you like to stay for something, it won't take long to prepare.

Jacqui No, no thank you. Not for me. I ate earlier and I don't wish to add to the waistline unless absolutely necessary. But, please, don't let me stop you; you two must be starving having done all that travelling today.

Jenny Well if you don't mind, I will. Frank?

Frank Yes, darling, whatever.

Jenny exits to the cellar

Frank What happened while I was out?

Jacqui Oh! It was nothing. I came round to say hallo, I had a coat over my head to keep me from the rain and when Jenny opened the door she thought I was the bogeyman and fainted. Has she always been nervous?

Frank Jenny? The last thing I would have said about Jenny was that she was nervous.

Jacqui If you wanted, you could both stay at my place tonight. It could be fun, the three of us!

Frank pops the cork on the champagne bottle; he pours the drinks during the following

Frank Don't be silly, we're both fine. Besides I wouldn't want to leave the house empty.

Jacqui No, no, of course not; it was just an idea.

Frank Well, how about that drink? (*He hands a glass of champagne to Jacqui*)

Jacqui Bottoms up! I was just saying to Jenny how much I was looking forward to meeting you. She tells me you are very good at — having a good time. I do hope so. This village could do with some new life. I find it so dull at times and it's lovely to have some young people moving in.

Frank Why? Were the previous tenants old fuddy-duddies?

Jacqui The previous tenants? Oh, the people before you! Well, I don't really know, you see; I only moved in myself not so long ago so I didn't get the chance to meet them.

Frank Where were you before that? The big city, I presume.

Jacqui Yes, that's right, we were from town. Listen, I must make a move. I'm expecting a call to meet someone later. I'm sorry to dash. I didn't realize the time. (*She calls*) Bye, Jenny. See you over the weekend, perhaps? Goodbye Frank, do say goodbye to Jenny. I expect she can't hear me from down there.

Frank OK Jacqui. Hope to have the pleasure again soon.

Jacqui The pleasure, I hope, will be mine!

Jacqui exits, slowly closing the door after herself

Frank pours himself a glass of champagne, sits down and picks up a magazine from the table. He begins to read. After a moment he stops, listening

Frank Jenny ... Jenny ...

Jenny enters with a plate of cheese sandwiches

Jenny You yelled!

Frank What's that?

Jenny Supper.

Frank Supper?

Jenny Correct.

Frank But why?

Jenny Because dear old Mrs Gregory has stocked the fridge up with cheese and milk, bread and eggs, but has somehow locked the freezer and not left the key. I have hunted high and low but I can't get into that damn thing. You hate eggs and therefore the alternatives were somewhat limited. So this is supper.

Frank Champagne and cheese sandwiches. Isn't married life bliss!

Jenny It won't be if you leave me alone in the house again when the lights go out.

Frank I'm sorry, darling. I didn't realize the power would get cut again. The lights are on now though. What was the problem?

Jenny I never found out. I went to telephone the operator for the Electricity Board's number but never got through. I got so frightened. Look, Frank, I passed out. I thought I saw some sort of hideous thing at the door. Now don't laugh because it gave me one hell of a shock.

Frank I don't think Jacqui is that bad!

Jenny I think I'm just jet-lagged. My imagination's playing tricks.

Frank I know, she told me. In fact I think she's after my body. Even invited us to spend the night at her house.

Jenny She suggested to me that we should go away for the weekend. Frank, I nearly said yes.

Frank Let me remind you it was you who wanted to move in here so badly. It was ideal and perfect, very homely *et cetera, et cetera.* What's made you change your mind?

Jenny I didn't say I had changed my mind. Now Jacqui has told me that there are burglars in the village I just feel a bit uneasy, that's all. I'll be all right after a good night's sleep.

Frank That's funny, she never mentioned burglars to me. I wonder why? You go up. Just let me finish this feast.

Jenny goes up the stairs and exits into the dressing-room

Frank finishes his glass of champagne and moves over to the front door. He opens it and looks out, then, looking satisfied that no-one is to be seen, he closes and bolts it. He then goes to the french windows, pulls back the curtains, checks the door lock and closes the curtains. He then picks up the champagne bottle, the magazine and two glasses and takes them up to the bedroom, putting them on the table next to the bed. He pours champagne into the glasses

Jenny enters from the dressing-room dressed for bed. She gets into the bed and Frank hands her a glass of champagne

Frank Welcome to our new home, Mrs Gilman.
Jenny Frank, I don't think I should drink this. I still feel queasy.
Frank Come on, let's drink a toast to us — please!
Jenny Oh, all right, I suppose it will help me sleep.
Frank Sleep! Who said anything about sleep?
Jenny You have a one-track mind, Frank.
Frank I know. Isn't it just disgusting? But, that's why you married me!
Jenny Go and get ready for bed, Casanova. How much of this bottle have you had?

Frank exits to the dressing-room

Frank (*off*) It wasn't just me. Anyway, Jumping Jaq Flash next door helped me with the bottle when you were in the kitchen preparing that feast of a supper to welcome me home from the lashing rain and howling wind.
Jenny Don't be so dramatic, Frank.
Frank (*imitating Jacqui*) I am not dramatic, darling. Mind you, with you passing out and the theatrical man-eater next door, it just seems to be the norm round here. I'm just glad I married you and not her next door. I wonder what her husband must be like. Poor sod probably only moved here to keep her quiet.
Jenny Leave poor Jacqui alone — and anyway she's divorced. She must have seen all sorts move in and out of here. I think it was a really kind gesture for her to make the first move and visit us. She must be sick of it after twelve years, seeing people come and go.

Frank appears in the doorway wearing a dressing-gown

Frank Twelve years? What do you mean? She's only been here a short while.
Jenny No, no Frank, she got divorced twelve years ago, which is why she moved to the village in the first place, on the settlement money.

Frank I could have sworn she said ... hang on, that's right. I asked her
what the people were like that lived here before us and she said she
didn't know because she only moved in a short while ago.
Jenny You've got hold of the wrong end of the stick. That and a few too
many glasses.
Frank I'll prove just how much the booze has affected me in a moment.

They kiss

*A black-clad figure (Mr Watson) emerges from behind the curtains to
the french windows*

*The underscore begins. The figure moves slowly across the room towards
the cellar door. Just as he passes the sofa the telephone rings. He ducks
down under the stairs*

Frank Who on earth is that?
Jenny I'll answer it. I'm coming.
Frank If only.

*Jenny makes her way downstairs, switching on the light at the side table.
She sits on the sofa and answers the telephone*

Jenny (*into the phone*) Mum, lovely, yes. ... Yes ... yes ... yes ... yes.
Yes, Mum, everything is fine. ... OK, well let me talk to you tomorrow
and see how the day goes. I'll speak to you then. Thanks ... look after
yourself ... bye. (*She runs back upstairs and gets into bed*)
Frank Your mum's timing always was incomparable. What did she want
... this time ... she only rang a few hours ago.

*The figure reappears from behind the stairs and exits through the cellar
door during the following*

Jenny Just leave her out of it.
Frank I didn't invite her in. Now give us a kiss.

*They embrace again. There is a noise from the cellar. Frank and Jenny
freeze*

Jenny Frank. Did you ...

Frank Ssh.

Frank goes down the stairs and looks around. He moves to the french windows and looks out through the curtains. Jenny moves slowly to the edge of the stairs to look down into the living area. Frank moves round the room to the stained-glass window and then suddenly turns to face the cellar door, as if he has heard a noise

The underscore begins to get faster and more menacing

Frank moves slowly towards the door. As he reaches it, a black-gloved hand punches through the small glass window in the door and grabs him by the throat. Frank splutters and struggles and eventually pushes the door inwards. He struggles with the figure behind the door; as they emerge we see that the figure is carrying a blood-stained ice cooler box which apparently contains something heavy. In the struggle the figure kicks Frank in the face and then runs past him and out of the french windows as ——

—— the CURTAIN *falls*

ACT II

SCENE 1

The same. The next morning

The curtains are open and light streams through the windows. Jacqui Henderson and Jenny are sitting on the sofa. Jenny is curled up wearing a dressing-gown. The champagne bottle is now on the dressing table in the bedroom

Jenny I really don't know how to thank you, Jacqui. I mean, we hardly know you — and just coming round like that in the middle of the night.

Jacqui Well, darling, when I saw the police car arrive with everything flashing ... you know I can't resist a man in a uniform so of course I had to come round to find out what was going on. It was purely selfish, darling.

Jenny I suppose running Frank to casualty was selfish too.

Jacqui Absolutely. Spending the night with that good-looking fellow was a joy. They're all so old and unexciting round here. It makes a change to sit round casualty with a young man. Anyway, how is he this morning?

Jenny He's got a bit of a headache but he's really no worse for wear. The biggest headache was giving the statement to the police. They wanted to know everything in such detail. The odd thing is, Jacqui, they didn't seem to know anything about the other burglaries in the village.

Jacqui Oh, darling, it's the sign of the times. Crime is even reaching little outposts like Milbury nowadays and the police don't know what goes on. What chance do we all have?

Jenny But that's just the point. Nothing was stolen, yet he ran past me carrying something. I tell you, this is so bizarre. I mean, we've only been here a day. Why didn't they have the courtesy to break in before we arrived?

Jacqui Darling, even the common criminal has lost all sense of what is right and wrong. They think of no-one but themselves. Whatever happened to good manners?

Jenny More coffee?

Jacqui No thank you, darling, I really must be going. Listen, why don't you and Frank come over for the afternoon?

Jenny That's very kind of you but we've got a bit to do before we return to work on Monday.

Jacqui OK. But I'll be in all afternoon if you change your mind. Now I must be off.

Jenny Yes, of course. Frank will be back soon anyway. He only popped out to buy some bits and pieces from the DIY shop.

Jacqui Yes, I expect he's very good with his hands. Listen, must rush. Give my love to Frank.

Jacqui exits

Jenny picks up the cups. There is the sound of a car pulling up outside. Jenny goes to the french windows and then to the front door, which she opens, with some difficulty

Frank enters; he has a plaster on his head and is carrying two plastic bags of shopping and a toolkit

Jenny Hallo, soldier. (*She hugs Frank*) You've just missed Jacqui.

Frank Oh. What did she want?

Jenny She just popped in to see if I was all right. She asked us round for the afternoon, said it would do us good to get out for a few hours, but I said we had too much to do.

Frank I think she is definitely a bit strange. She's either making suggestive remarks or trying to get us out of the house. Anyway, I've got a busy afternoon. I bought the new telephone plus extension kit for the bedroom upstairs and a new lock for the french windows and some shopping.

Jenny Good. Now you get on with that and I'll make some more coffee. How do you feel?

Frank I'm OK now but I had a splitting headache earlier.

Jenny picks up the food shopping and exits to the kitchen

Frank picks up the tools and sets to work on the french windows

A figure — Mr Harvey — appears outside the french windows

Frank puts down his tools and slowly opens the doors

Frank May I ask what you're doing?

Mr Harvey Just a spot o' diggin' out back. It's just I heard there was a bit of trouble round here last night and was just checkin' up on you, so to speak. I didn't mean to intrude, sir.

Frank That seems to be the norm around here — people intruding. You must be Harvey, Mr Harvey — Miss Peterson told me about you. You look after the grounds round here, don't you?

Mr Harvey Amongst other things, sir, yes, I do.

Frank Listen, we're just making coffee; would you like a cup?

Mr Harvey Don't mind if I do, sir. That's very kind of you.

Frank You must know Miss Henderson, Jacqui Henderson, next door?

Mr Harvey Oh, yes, sir, I know her, she's very good to me. Always looks after me when I'm working.

Frank How long has she been around? I mean, how long has she lived at the chapel?

Mr Harvey Well, sir, that is a question. Let me see ...

Jenny enters, carrying a cup of coffee

Jenny Frank, here's your coffee. (*To Mr Harvey*) Oh, hallo.

Frank Jenny, this is our gardener, Mr Harvey. He was just telling me about how long Jacqui Henderson had lived round here.

Jenny Would you like a cup of coffee, Mr Harvey?

Mr Harvey That's very kind of you, Miss.

Jenny Milk and sugar?

Frank Thank you kindly, Miss.

Jenny exits to the kitchen

Frank So you were saying, Mr Harvey — about next door ...

Mr Harvey Oh, yes, sir. Well, I'd say that Miss Henderson's been there for some years, about twelve or so.

Frank So you would see a lot of people come and go over the years. I mean, who was here before we were?

Mr Harvey That I couldn't tell you, sir. They tended to keep themselves to themselves. They worked odd hours sir, always very late, and therefore I didn't hardly see 'em at all.

Frank So where do you live, Mr Harvey?

Mr Harvey Oh, I have a small cottage which belongs to the Church, sir.

I get it for next to no rent because I do a bit of digging for them every now and then.

Frank You look after the gardens?

Mr Harvey Well, it's more digging than gardening, sir, if you know what I mean. I'm doing a bit of digging for them now, in the graveyard.

Frank Oh, I see, *that* sort of digging. Who are you digging for at the moment? I mean, who has died?

Mr Harvey I don't rightly know, sir, we wasn't formally introduced! All that happens is the vicar, the Reverend Parker, gives me the date and I digs the hole. A lot of them don't have much fancy gubbins or anything like that. Them that's posh gets buried nearer the church.

Jenny enters with another cup of coffee

Jenny (*handing the cup to Mr Harvey*) There you go, Mr Harvey. If you'll excuse me I'm going to get dressed. Frank, can I have a word a minute?

Mr Harvey I'd better get on. I'll take my coffee with me, Miss, if you don't mind. I'll return the cup.

Frank That's no problem. We'll see you later perhaps?

Mr Harvey exits through the french windows

Frank What's wrong, Jenny?

Jenny The freezer, that's what's wrong.

Frank I know; you told me it was locked last night.

Jenny Well, it may have been last night but it is unlocked today.

Frank Well, maybe you just didn't lift hard enough, or maybe it was stuck.

Jenny No, Frank, it was definitely locked. But not just that — it's empty. There isn't a single crumb of meat or anything in that freezer at all.

Frank Jenny, I can't believe we were broken into in order to steal a dozen lamb chops and some frozen peas. Things are tough but this is ridiculous. Maybe Mrs Gregory didn't do any shopping at all. It was emptied ready for the next occupants who happened to be us.

Jenny Well, if that was the case how was it locked yesterday and unlocked today?

Frank I told you, maybe it was stiff. As I said, you probably didn't try hard enough.

Jenny There is something wrong, I know it. And while we're on about locked doors: we still haven't had a key for this cupboard door. I wonder what secret lies behind there?

Frank We did ask John Watson to bring a key round. I expect he'll bring it next week if he's passing.

Jenny Ring him, Frank, and ask him to bring it round. Estate agents are usually open on a weekend. We do need the space.

Frank All right. But then I must finish these locks on the french doors and you want this extension fitted. If you make a sandwich, I'll telephone Watson.

Jenny It's a deal.

Jenny exits to the kitchen

Frank picks up the phone and dials

Frank (*into the phone*) Hallo, hallo ... oh, a damn machine. Hallo, this is Frank Gilman at the chapel. I wonder if you had any luck with the key to the cupboard door and perhaps you could drop it in as soon as possible. Thank you. (*He hangs up. He picks up his tools and sets to work on the french windows once more, then stops and goes over to the locked cupboard door and tries to unlock it. He crosses the room, picks up a screwdriver, returns to the door and tries to unscrew the door handle*)

The underscore begins

Mr Harvey appears in the french windows with his coffee cup

Mr Harvey I wouldn't do that if I were you, sir!

Frank (*turning round suddenly*) Oh, God, you gave me a shock. That's the second time you've done that today.

Mr Harvey I was just returning your cup, sir.

Frank Just leave it on the table. You wouldn't do what if you were me?

Mr Harvey (*putting the cup on the table*) Break open the door or whatever you're doing.

Frank The door won't open.

Mr Harvey That's because it's locked, sir.

Frank I realize that. I am trying to get it open.

Frank turns to look at the door, with his back to Mr Harvey. During the following, Mr Harvey circles round the room, moving towards Frank and playing menacingly with a large handkerchief pulled from his pocket

The underscore builds in intensity

Mr Harvey Why don't you use a key, sir? That estate agent chap should have a copy of everything. That's what I was told. They had copies of all the keys for this place.

Frank Well, they haven't come up with a key for this door yet so I'm going to try and get it open it myself. Actually you wouldn't like to give me a hand with this? The heads on these screws seem to have worn. I can't get the screwdriver to hold.

Mr Harvey closes in on Frank ...

The underscore fades

Mr Harvey mops his brow with the handkerchief

Harvey Would be more than my job's worth, sir. I can't be seen to be defacing property that don't belong to me. I suggest you do the same, otherwise you'll be charged for damage.

Frank I was hoping somebody else would be charged for damaging me last night. Oh, I guess you're right. Jenny will just have to wait for this cupboard space. Seems odd to keep it locked though.

Harvey I must be going, sir. Thank you for the coffee once again.

Frank You're welcome, Mr Harvey. See you tomorrow, perhaps?

Mr Harvey Oh, no, sir. Sundays are my days at the church across the village. But I'll be around next week, I expect.

Frank Do you mind if I have a go at the front lawn tomorrow then?

Mr Harvey Be my guest, sir. I won't get round to it till next week anyhow. I'll leave the gardening tools by the shed if you like.

Frank See you next week then?

Mr Harvey Goodbye, sir.

Mr Harvey exits

Frank closes the french windows

Jenny enters from the kitchen carrying a tray of sandwiches which she places on the table by the sofa

Jenny Ooh, it's getting a bit cold in here. Can we have the fire lit?

Frank It's just because I've had the door open to old Mr Harvey. It will soon warm up.

Jenny Go on. It will be so cosy with a fire in here. I can tell Mr Harvey has just gone. I'm sure he smells, you know.

Frank I noticed it when I was standing right next to him. Anyway, he is a gardener; what do you expect?

Jenny Open the window a few minutes. You do notice it when you come into this room.

Frank You've just said you're cold. Make up your mind. What's it to be?

Jenny If you go and get the logs then you can leave the doors open to clear the smell.

Frank You don't mind if I have something to eat between opening the doors, getting the logs, mending the doors, running around with air fresheners, putting the new telephone in and whistling "Hi ho, hi ho!" as I go?

Jenny Frank, I remember a conversation yesterday that had me scrubbing shirts, shopping and ironing whilst you sat round handing out the orders.

Frank Do I feel a domestic scene coming on?

Jenny No, as long as you do what you're told. Eat now.

Frank Yes, boss.

They both start to eat lunch at the small table in front of the sofa

You're quite lucky really.

Jenny Why's that?

Frank You've got a housemaid, a gardener and a slave called Frank.

Jenny You are the limit sometimes. Now eat. We've got a lot to do today.

Frank Why, what are you going to do?

Jenny I'm going to do some baking. I may as well fill that freezer up with something.

Frank If I get a chance to get through your list of jobs, I'm going to have a go at that front lawn tomorrow. Harvey said he'd leave his stuff by the shed.

Jenny I don't understand what he does. He can't be very good if you have to do his job for him. I mean, where else does he work?

Frank He told me he did some work at the church across the village on Sundays. And he's supposed to look after next door's garden. I guess he's like the village odd job man.

Jenny I hope we're not paying for his services full time then, especially if you end up having to do his odd jobs.

Frank I don't mind. I enjoy a little bit of gardening now and again, if it helps him out. Anyway, you're doing some baking. What happened to Mrs Gregory? We were told you'd end up doing next to nothing in the kitchen. She's supposed to look after the cooking and cleaning.

Jenny It is the weekend, Frank. We'll see her on Monday.

Frank Hang on. That's right. Didn't you leave list of shopping with the agents so there'd be food for our return?

Jenny What's that got to do with anything?

Frank Where do you usually put the meat — but the freezer.

Jenny Of course. But I don't understand. The freezer was locked after Miss Peterson went and today it is unlocked and there's nothing there. I swear the lid wasn't stuck, Frank — that freezer was locked.

Frank So what does that make our intruders, hard-up butchers? Miss Peterson didn't take the meat with her on Friday. Unless Mrs Gregory didn't do all the shopping.

Jenny We'll ask her on Monday. Can you imagine if we have to tell the police we lost a leg of lamb and a dozen pork chops?

They finish eating and Frank gets up and opens the french windows

Frank Let me go and see if there are any logs outside.

Frank exits

Jenny clears the table

Frank returns with a couple of logs

Jenny That's not going to last very long. Is that all there is?

Frank I'm afraid so. I am sure there must be a saw lying around somewhere. Let me see if I can get this going first.

Jenny exits with the tray

Frank goes over to the fireplace and tries to light a fire. He takes a newspaper from the table and uses it as kindling, but all he manages to achieve is smoke which seems to persist

Jenny returns

Jenny I guess that's one way of getting rid of a smell. Frank, what are you
    doing?
Frank Jen, I think this chimney must be blocked. It's not drawing the
    flames at all.

*They carry the grate out of the fireplace so that Frank can put his head up
the chimney. He sits down*

Are you absolutely determined to have a fire today?
Jenny It would be good to try and get one going.
Frank Can't you just have the central heating on today?

Jenny looks firmly at Frank

(*With resignation*) All right. Go and find me something to poke up this
    chimney. It seems to be blocked a couple of feet up.
Jenny What do you want, a stick or handle of something?
Frank Yes. Bring me a spade or something. It will be in the shed.

Jenny exits

*Frank gets up inside the chimney to look again, then emerges, picks up
more newspapers from the table and screws them up for a further attempt*

*Jenny enters carrying a spade. It is covered in blood, although Jenny
has not yet noticed this. Frank does not turn to face her as she comes in*

Jenny I found this.
Frank Good. That'll do.
Jenny (*suddenly noticing the blood*) Frank, wait, look at my hands! God,
    what is it? They're all red and ... Frank, get it off me, get it off. It's blood,
    fresh blood!

Music plays as ——

—— *the* CURTAIN *falls*

SCENE 2

Sunday: late afternoon

As well as the phone in the living-room, there is a new extension phone in the bedroom. The phone is ringing and there is a knocking at the door as the CURTAIN rises

Jenny enters from the kitchen; Frank enters from the bathroom upstairs

Jenny I'll get the phone if you get the door. (*She answers the phone*)

Frank goes to the front door and tries to open it; it is stuck, however

Frank (*shouting*) I'm sorry, but you'll have to push. It's stuck.
Jenny (*referring to the phone call*) Frank, I'm going to take this upstairs.
Frank Hang on a bit, love. I can't get this damn door open.

The door bursts open and Mr Watson enters

Jenny Hallo, Mr Watson. As you can see, we are having problems with the front door. It keeps getting stuck. Frank, will you put the receiver down when I yell? (*She heads upstairs and picks up the phone receiver during the following*)
Frank (*to Mr Watson*) Yes, I'm sorry, but this door seems to be getting worse.
Mr Watson Please don't apologize. I feel guilty. I should have someone come round and plane the door. It seems a shame because it's such a lovely old door. Leave it with me, I'll get someone on to it in the morning. I'd get old Harvey to look at it but he's across at the church on Sundays.
Jenny (*calling down*) Frank, will you hang up for me, please?
Frank (*hanging up the downstairs receiver; to Mr Watson*) Well, I wanted to talk to you about Harvey.
Mr Watson Oh, yes, and what's that about? I hope he hasn't been making a nuisance of himself?
Frank I think it could be slightly more serious than that. You see, we found this spade which we presume he uses — it's covered in blood.
Mr Watson Are you sure? I mean, it could be ——
Frank It's blood. Most of it was dried on.

Mr Watson All I was going to say was that it could be blood from a rabbit or a mole or indeed rats. There is an enormous number of rodents in the country, Mr Gilman, you know. I recall Harvey has mentioned it to me before. He's no doubt caught a few in his time. It certainly is an effective way of dealing with the little vermin.

Frank (*laughing*) You must be joking?

Mr Watson I'm serious. They can be a hell of a nuisance.

Frank Please, for God's sake don't mention it to Jenny. She'll be out of here as soon as look at a rat.

Mr Watson Don't worry about it. It is quite usual. There isn't a plague of them. Ironically, you'll probably find more in the city than you will in the country. It's important you don't leave any scraps around in the rubbish. That's bound to attract all sorts of unwelcome visitors.

Frank I'll bear that in mind. Anyway, if you could get Harvey to come round it would be useful. I'm back at work tomorrow but Jenny will be around. I guess you rarely get any time off nowadays in your trade.

Mr Watson It's not as bad as it seems. We're not overburdened with work, as you can imagine, at the moment, so the weeks are usually quite quiet. That way I can shut up shop every so often. The answerphone takes any messages, or Miss Peterson. It's the weekends that are the worst. People down from the city looking for holiday or retirement cottages and the like. I've only just finished and the day is nearly gone.

Frank No peace for the wicked, eh?

Mr Watson You could say that!

Frank Can I offer you a glass of something, or a coffee?

Mr Watson That's kind of you but I think I'll pass on this occasion. I just stopped off on my way home. I left Miss Peterson to lock up as she still had some clients with her.

Frank Mr Watson, what happened to the previous tenants?

Mr Watson That's a strange question. What makes you ask?

Frank Curiosity really. It's just that no-one has any idea where they moved on to.

Mr Watson It wasn't a "they", it was a "he". I forget his name. Businessman like yourself. Didn't stay long, a couple of months as far as I can recall. I am sure we'll have a contact number for him should you want it.

Frank That's odd. A man who left here only a week ago; surely you can't have forgotten his name so soon?

Mr Watson We do deal with quite a lot of clients, Mr Gilman. I haven't actually forgotten it, but it was a strange name, foreign. Cassiopi, yes, that's it, Cassiopi.

Frank Cassiopi, well I'll tell Jenny. She was more interested than I was.

Jenny comes down the stairs

Jenny What was I interested in?

Frank We were just discussing who was here before us. Apparently it was a businessman.

Jenny Well, perhaps someone would call him and ask for the key to that cupboard. What was his name?

Mr Watson I was just saying. It was a foreign name, a Mr Cassiopi.

Frank Is that why you've come by, to give us the key?

Mr Watson No, I called round to see what you wanted. The answer-machine cut off halfway through your call to me, so I thought I would call in and find out.

Frank I see. Well, it's the key, we need it. Have you found it, yet?

Mr Watson Ah, yes, I asked Miss Peterson to sort this out for you. I take it she hasn't been in touch?

Frank No. I know, why don't you call her now before she leaves? She could drop it in tonight.

Mr Watson Yes, good idea. May I use your phone? (*He picks up the phone and dials. He waits a while*) Oh, yes, it's me. I'm at the Gilmans'. What's happening regarding this lost key? ... Yes, yes, that's fine. ... All right, I'll let them know. (*He hangs up. To Frank*) You're in luck. A new key has been cut as the last one was snapped by using it in the wrong lock. Miss Peterson says she will pick it up tomorrow and drop it in.

Frank I won't be here but Jenny will be. You're not going out, are you, darling?

Jenny I have some work to do, that's all. Mother is meeting me in town. I can delay her until after lunch if you like.

Mr Watson No, please don't. Miss Peterson can deliver it at the end of the day, after work. I really don't want to inconvenience you.

Frank That's fine then. Thanks for coming round, Mr Watson, and sorting that out. Do you know, for a moment I thought you didn't want us using that cupboard.

Mr Watson I'd best be going. Good to see you again. Good-night.

Jenny Thanks again. Goodbye!

Mr Watson exits

Frank and Jenny watch him leave, then close the front door

I had better give Mother a ring back and bring our lunch forward, just to be on the safe side, then I'll be back by five.

Jenny picks up the phone receiver and dials a number

Frank goes up the stairs and exits to the bathroom

I can't get a tone. The line can't be down. I don't understand. This phone seems totally dead. (*She hangs up and then tries dialling again*) I only used this five minutes ago. (*She calls*) Frank, there's something wrong with the line. Frank!
Frank (*off*) What's wrong?
Jenny I can't get a line. There is no dialling tone.

Frank enters from the bathroom and goes to the telephone by the bed

Frank Guess who didn't replace the receiver properly? (*He hangs up the bedroom phone*)
Jenny That's it. I've got a tone now. (*She dials*)

Frank exits to the bathroom again

Jenny stops dialling, replaces the receiver and runs upstairs as she calls the following. The underscore begins

Frank, Frank.

Frank enters

Frank What now, Jenny?
Jenny Don't you realize what that means?
Frank What does what mean? Jen, calm down.
Jenny Frank, who the hell was Watson talking to on the telephone?
Frank I assume Miss Peterson. He said he was going to bring the key round tomorrow. I don't think anyone else works in his office.
Jenny No, not Miss Peterson, not anyone! How could he if the extension was off the hook? He had no dialling tone.
Frank But why, Jen? Why does he go to all this trouble, pretending to talk

to someone, telling us the old key was broken and a new one was being cut? Why all these lies? I know, one last check — let me try calling his office.

Frank picks up the phone, dials and waits

I thought as much. The answerphone is on again. She probably wasn't there at all today.

Jenny Then why lie about it?

Frank I don't know. Maybe he forgot all about the key, forgot to tell Miss Peterson and didn't like to tell us. I did push him about the key. It's strange but I got the feeling he didn't want us using this cupboard.

Jenny Frank, there is something strange going on. I am sure of it. All that bit about not remembering who was here before us, and now all this.

Frank I agree, but I'm not sure what we do about it.

Jenny Maybe nothing, but there seems to be a reluctance to give us any information on the past. It's as though everyone seems to be protecting something or someone.

Frank Damn. I meant to mention the blocked chimney to him.

Jenny I've got it. Why don't I ring the operator and ask for customer services? They'll have a record of the name.

Frank If you do that, I'm going to get that spade and see if I can clear that blockage in the chimney.

Frank exits through the french windows

Jenny dials the operator

Jenny (*into the phone*) Hallo, can you put me through to Customer Services. ... Hallo, I wonder if you can help me. My name is Gilman, Jenny Gilman. We've just moved in and taken over this number from the previous tenant. We've got some mail for him, but don't have a forwarding address. His name is Cassiopi, the number is six-o-seven-three. ... Yes, thank you. ... Yes, I'll hold. ... Hallo ... are you sure? But that's not possible. ... I mean ... well, thank you for your help. (*She hangs up*) Frank!

Frank returns with a stick

I just spoke with the telephone operator. No-one with the name Cassiopi has ever been listed here!

Frank But I'm sure he said ...

Jenny He did, and he lied, lied for the third time.

Frank So where does that put us?

Jenny Nowhere at all. It's just a lot of unanswered questions.

Frank Not really. We can't get the cupboard door open and we found blood on a spade.

Jenny Did you ask Mr Watson about that?

Frank Um — yes, he said he knew nothing about it and he'd question Harvey about it next week.

Jenny Is that all? I thought he might have shown rather more concern than that.

Frank OK, but if I tell you what he said, promise me you won't get hysterical.

Jenny I do not get hysterical. What did he say?

Frank He reckoned it was rats.

Jenny Rats?

Frank Yes. There are a few rats and moles and rabbits around which Harvey knocks off with this spade.

Jenny begins to laugh

Now Jen, don't get hysterical. You said you wouldn't get hysterical.

Jenny I'm not hysterical. I just think it's hysterically funny. Can you imagine old Mr Harvey taking swipes at these so-called rats? He wouldn't stand a chance. Really, Frank, I've never heard such rubbish. He's far too slow.

Frank In that case, I don't know what you find so funny. What or whose blood was it on this spade?

Jenny Maybe you should go over and ask him. You said he's over at the church on Sundays.

Frank I will, but let me have a go with this chimney first and see if I can get it cleared.

Jenny All right. (*She laughs*) I can still picture this scene with Harvey chasing the rats.

Frank Come on, give me a hand.

Frank goes over to the chimney breast and pushes the spade handle up the chimney; we hear a deadly thudding sound

It seems fairly stubborn. (*Pause*) Oh, my God, it's soft. (*He stops prodding with the spade and sits down in front of the fireplace*)

Jenny What is it? What's up there?

Frank I don't know, but it feels soft and smooth. Maybe I should leave it there.

Jenny Don't be so stupid. Whatever it is, it has to come down. I'm not sitting in this room not knowing what thing is trapped up there. Come on, we've got to get it out or we'll never be able to use this fireplace.

Frank OK. Hold this. (*He gives Jenny the spade*) I think I can reach it now.

Frank goes back into the chimney, crouching so that his head and shoulders disappear from view

The underscore begins

Jenny Be careful. Watch you don't hurt yourself.

Frank It's coming.

Jenny Can you get a hold of it?

Frank I think so. Hang on, Jen. Get me a torch, can you?

Jenny picks up the torch from under the table and moves to pass it to Frank

(*Yelling in panic*) Aargh! Jen, help. Aargh!

Jenny Frank, what —what's wrong?

Frank comes out of the chimney and sits on the floor; his face and mouth are covered in soot

Frank I'm sorry, but I took a mouthful of soot. God, that tastes foul. Give me the torch.

Jenny hands Frank the torch and he goes back into the chimney, his head and shoulders disappearing from view

Jenny Is that better? Can you see anything?

Frank Not really. I can't get hold of it with the torch in my hand. Can you hold it and shine it up?

Frank passes the torch down to Jenny, who kneels by him, attempting to assist. There is a loud thud. Frank falls down. Dust, then a soot-stained laundry bag, fall down on him

The underscore stops

Jenny Are you all right?
Frank I think so. (*He looks back up the chimney*) Well, that seems to have cleared it.
Jenny (*looking at the laundry bag*) What's inside this? God, it looks revolting!
Frank Just some bag to block the chimney. It was probably put there to stop the draught. Mr Cassiopi or whatever his name was didn't like open fires. (*He gets up and makes his way up the stairs*) I'm just going to get this muck off me.

Frank exits through the bathroom door

Jenny opens the laundry bag and empties it on to the floor; the contents — a man's clothes — are covered in bloodstains

Jenny Our friend obviously didn't like wearing clothes. These are someone's trousers, shirt, jumper. (*She yells*) Frank, you'd better take a look at these.

Frank appears, wiping his face with a damp towel. He comes down the stairs during the following

Frank What have you found, Jen?
Jenny Come here and look at these things. You wouldn't use clothes to block the draught. These are his clothes, Frank.
Frank They're probably old clothes. But whose clothes?
Jenny This Mr Cassiopi. There's a full outfit here, including his socks!
Frank Let me see. (*He examines the clothing*) Look at that stain on the jumper. That's blood, I think.
Jenny Give it to me. Yes, Frank, that is dried blood, I'm sure. And look at these rags ...
Frank What shall we do with these now?
Jenny Hang on, let me check the pockets. (*She searches through the pockets of the trousers; in one is a screwed-up piece of paper*) What's this? (*She throws the piece of paper down and continues to search*)
Frank (*picking up the discarded paper and reading it*) Jen, look at this.
Jenny What?
Frank This is an old Visa receipt. It's for a meal at some restaurant —

eighty-seven pounds! Can't be anywhere round here. Mr G. Rosman. That's it! G. Rosman was our businessman.

Jenny How do you know it's our businessman?

Frank It seems to be the sort of amount you'd spend entertaining a client or someone. Who else spends eighty-seven pounds on lunch?

Jenny It could be dinner.

Frank No, it says it was for lunch at the Royal Hotel.

Jenny Let's check the jacket.

They search the jacket and discover nothing

Let's get this lot back in the bag. At least we've got a name.

Frank (*referring to the laundry bag*) You hold it open while I put this lot back in.

Jenny (*pulling an envelope out of the laundry bag*) What's this?

Frank Open it then.

Jenny All right. Hang on. (*She opens the envelope and removes several sheets of paper from it*) What on earth are these?

Frank and Jenny share out the sheets of paper

Frank These are from a hospital, I think.

Jenny No they're not. It's from his doctor. Frank, these are medical records. Look, there are reports on illness, insurance, medicals, the lot, all relating to a G. Rosman.

Frank George, that was his first name — look, it's on this report here.

Jenny Why would he have his own medical reports?

Frank But he wouldn't. I think it's obvious he didn't place this up the chimney. Someone else did. But why?

Jenny Frank, I'm scared. This doesn't make sense. What happened to George Rosman? This lot has been hidden. He couldn't get access to his medical files unless he was a doctor.

Frank He wasn't. According to Mr Watson he was a businessman. That's if we believe him.

The phone rings. Frank and Jenny look at each other tensely. The underscore starts

Jenny You answer it. Go on.

Frank picks up the receiver

Frank (*into the phone*) Hallo, six-o-seven-three. … Hallo, hallo … (*To Jenny*) They've hung up. (*He hangs up*)
Jenny That's the second time. Who do they want? Or are they just checking to see if somebody is in?
Frank I think I may just take a walk to see if I can find Mr Harvey. I've got some questions for him. He's supposed to be working at the church today. If I'm quick I may catch him. Stay here, Jenny. When I return I think it's time to call the police.
Jenny Don't be long, Frank. It will be dark soon.
Frank I won't, I promise.

Frank exits to the dressing room and returns carrying a coat; he makes his way downstairs and exits through the french windows

Jenny moves to the windows, looking out. There is a knocking at the door which continues through the following. Jenny spins round, frightened, and heads for the front door. She then turns and bundles the bloodstained clothes and papers into the laundry bag and puts the bag by the fireplace. She moves to the front door and tries to open it; again it is stuck

Jenny Who is it?

No reply. Jenny walks to the french windows and opens them

   Hallo. Who is there?

The underscore stops

Jacqui (*off*) It's me, darling.

Jacqui enters through the french windows

Jenny I'm sorry, you gave me a fright.
Jacqui Darling, you must get that front door fixed. It is a positive nuisance.
Jenny Someone is supposed to be coming this week in order to fix the thing.
Jacqui Listen, I only came round because your phone was constantly

engaged. I wanted to know if you would like to come into London with me tomorrow?

Jenny Jacqui, I'd love to but I'm meeting Mother to do some shopping. I promised I would.

Jacqui Oh, well, perhaps another time. You can't disappoint your mother, now, can you?

Jenny Jacqui, look, I know this may sound strange but …

Jacqui Darling, what is wrong? You sound quite flustered.

Jenny Look, Mr Watson, the agent for this place, has just pretended to make a call to his office. We know he didn't because the upstairs phone was off the hook. It just makes me very suspicious and uncomfortable. All we asked for was a key to that cupboard and there is all this intrigue.

Jacqui Darling, how very dramatic. Are you absolutely sure he couldn't get a line out with the phone off the hook?

Jenny I am positive. We just tried it. I just don't understand it. We just seem to be unlucky here. Since we moved in we've been attacked, cheated and lied to. What is it with this place?

Jacqui Calm down, darling. I'm sure it is nothing.

Jenny Well, if we don't get this damn door open tomorrow I'll break the thing down myself.

Jacqui I wouldn't do that, I'm sure it will be sorted out tomorrow. *(She indicates the laundry bag)* Been doing some cleaning?

Jenny No, no. Look, Jacqui. Don't say anything to anyone at the moment but I want you to look at these.

Jenny empties the bag of clothes on to the floor. Jacqui looks stunned for a moment

Jacqui Darling, it looks like a jumble sale. How — where did you find these?

Jenny You'll never believe it but …

Frank enters through the french windows

Frank *(out of breath)* Jenny — oh, hi, Jacqui — Jen, come here a minute, can you? There is something I want you to see. Will you excuse us a minute, Jacqui?

Jenny We won't be a minute. Frank, what is it?

Frank Just come here and I'll show you. It's in the graveyard.

Jacqui Don't worry about me, darling. I'll go and put the kettle on and make you some tea. (*She heads for the cellar door*)

Jenny and Frank exit through the french windows

Jacqui stops and returns to the bag of clothes. She starts to rifle through the contents and finds the medical records

Oh shit! (*She puts the clothes back as they were but then discovers the Visa receipt lying on the floor*) Damn, damn — (*she thumps the nearest bit of furniture*) — damn! (*She grabs the phone and dials, then speaks*) It's me. Time has run out. They've found Rosman's clothes.... They're about to break into the cupboard. You'd better do something right away before they start shouting police. The operation has to be brought forward — and it's got to happen tonight.

Music

CURTAIN

SCENE 3

The same. Later that night

The door to the kitchen is ajar. Frank is in the bedroom, talking on the phone; he is wearing a dressing-gown

Frank (*into the phone*) Yes, I know all that. What I really would like is some information. ... But why can't you let me know tonight?... Well, when will he be available to talk? ... I don't think you understand. ... Yes, I do appreciate what time it is. ... Well, can't you go to the files and look it up for me?... I simply need to know the cause of death. ... I don't know, that's why I'm asking you. ... George Rosman ... that's right ... *Rosman*. ... No, I am not related. ... Because he's buried in the graveyard next to where he used to live. ... That is correct. ... I live here now. ... Very well, good-night. (*He hangs up*) Bloody bureaucratic copper.

Jenny enters from the kitchen in her night attire, carrying two mugs of tea. She switches off the downstairs lights and then makes her way up the stairs

Jenny Did you have any luck?

Frank No, as you might expect. The duty officer for the night has no access to the files and the officer who has isn't on duty till the morning so we still can't prove the previous tenant has ended up in the chapel graveyard. What the hell is going on here?

Jenny Maybe it's totally unconnected.

Frank Jenny, you saw for yourself. It's an old grave that's been freshly dug over. Why hasn't somebody said anything?

Jenny Why would somebody bury him here and not at the churchyard?

Frank And why didn't Harvey say anything, and Jacqui? I can't believe she missed out on that one. And where did she disappear to?

Jenny We were gone some time. Maybe she got bored and went. I can't see why that's important.

Frank I know something dodgy is going on.

Jenny Yes, I think you're right, but there's nothing to be done tonight so let's get a good night's sleep and get some answers tomorrow. I'll have a talk to Jacqui if you like and you can ring the agents. Deal?

Frank I reckon old hawk-eye next door must know something; perhaps I should ring her and ask her straight out.

Jenny You can't ring her in the middle of the night. Not everyone is awake this time of night.

Frank exits to the dressing room. He returns with jeans, a jumper and shoes and quickly gets dressed

Jenny What on earth are you up to now?

Frank I'm getting dressed.

Jenny I can see that, Frank. What are you getting dressed for in the middle of the night?

Frank I'm going grave-robbing!

Jenny What?

Frank Stay here. I won't be long. (*He goes down the stairs and heads for the french windows*)

Jenny Have you taken leave of your senses? (*She follows Frank*) You'll get arrested. Frank, please don't do this, not now. I don't understand why you want to dig up a dead body.

Frank (*turning and grabbing Jenny by the shoulders*) Because, Jenny, I
  believe George Rosman is buried in that grave and I've got to prove it.
  Go back to bed. I promise it won't take long!
Jenny How can I go to sleep with you out the back grave-robbing?
Frank I won't be long and I'm only outside.
Jenny Frank, it is the middle of the night and it's pouring with rain. If
  you're going, I might as well come with you. I can hold the torch or
  umbrella or something. (*She moves forward*)
Frank (*stopping Jenny*) There's no point in us both getting filthy.
Jenny Please be careful.

Frank exits

We must both be mad. (*She picks up a newspaper and matches and tries
to light the fire; the most she achieves, after several attempts, is a dim
glow and some smoke. She gives up and goes back upstairs*)

Jenny exits into the bathroom

The underscore begins

*A hand—that of Mr Watson—comes through the curtains which cover
the french windows. Mr Watson, dressed in dark colours and with his
face covered, enters, carrying a leather bag, which he places by the
staircase. He moves slowly to the cupboard door, brings a key out of his
pocket and unlocks the door. He goes into the cupboard, turning a light
on inside*

Jenny enters from the bathroom

Mr Watson freezes

*Jenny sits down at the dressing-table with her back to the audience and
begins to brush her hair*

*The telephone rings and Jenny moves to answer it. Mr Watson closes the
cupboard door quickly, leaving the light on; he freezes directly below
Jenny*

Jenny Hallo ... oh, hallo, officer. ... No, I'm afraid he's not here. ...

Where is he?... Well, yes. I'll tell him to ring you as soon as he gets back. ... Not at all, officer. ... Goodbye. (*She replaces the receiver*)

Mr Watson lifts the receiver on the phone downstairs and puts it down on the table next to the phone. He hides under the stairs

The underscore begins again

Who's there? Frank, is that you? Frank? (*She picks up the receiver again and dials, then stops, obviously realizing that there is no tone*) Hallo, hallo, is somebody there? (*She makes her way down the stairs*)

Mr Watson grabs Jenny's leg as she reaches the bottom of the stairs. She screams and runs back up to the bedroom, followed by Mr Watson

The underscore screams out

Mr Watson approaches Jenny. She throws the telephone at him and then picks up a can of hairspray from the dressing table and sprays it in his eyes. She then takes the empty champagne bottle from the dressing table and crashes it over Mr Watson's head. He collapses on to the bed and Jenny makes her escape down the stairs

During the following, Mr Watson gets up and exits to the bathroom

Jenny rushes to the french windows

A second masked figure — Jacqui Henderson — appears in the french windows with a knife in her hand

Jenny screams as Jacqui lunges towards her with the knife. Jenny grabs Jacqui's arm and forces it above their heads

Jenny forces Jacqui through the cellar door and locks it behind her. Thumping can be heard from behind the cellar door

Jenny heads back towards the french windows, preparing to call for help

Mr Watson enters through the french windows and blocks Jenny's path

Jenny screams and they struggle, Jenny digging her nails into Mr Watson's eyes; he yells. Recovering, Mr Watson pushes Jenny backwards.

She falls against the cupboard door which springs open to reveal the hanging mutilated body of George Rosman, or, rather, what remains of it

The underscore screams at high pitch at this point

Jenny makes a dash for the french windows

   Frank enters, covered in mud

Jenny screams again

Frank looks round the room as if assessing the situation. Mr Watson gets up and lunges towards Frank with the knife; Frank knocks the knife out of Mr Watson's hand and then strikes him unconscious, to lie still by the sofa

There is a considerable pause

Jenny Thank God you're all right. (*She indicates the body in the cupboard*) I think that's what remains of George Rosman.
Frank He's been cut open. What a mess. (*He sees Mr Watson's bag and moves to look more closely at it*) Jen, look at the name on it — Dr G. Harvey. Harvey?

They carefully open the case and extract the contents — a number of surgical instruments

   Look, it's full of knives and things. Like surgeon's knives. Oh, God, they've been operating, operating on Rosman.
Jenny There's nothing left of him.
Frank That's exactly it. His insides have been removed. His heart or his liver or whatever else was required.
Jenny What for? What on earth would be done with them?
Frank For money, Jen. They're selling human organs. How much would you pay for a transplant if it was a matter of life and death? (*He pulls a revolver from the bag and breaks it open*) A revolver! It appears it only has three bullets in it. I can hazard a guess at what happened to the other three.
Jenny (*finding a card*) Here's an old ID card. It's dated nineteen-eighty-seven. Look, here's a picture.
Frank My God, it's Watson.

Jenny But it's got Harvey's name.

Frank Who are one and the same. It makes sense. I've never seen them at the same time.

Jenny But why go to all that trouble? It doesn't make sense.

Frank It makes perfect sense. Harvey can come and go as he pleases. He operates on them as Dr Harvey, buries the victims under the guise of the gardener, whilst the Watson character does all the paperwork, lines up the tenants and mops up the mess.

Jenny Frank, what did we sign the other day, those so-called insurance forms. Did you read them?

Frank No, not properly. I wasn't really given a chance.

Jenny That's how they cover the burial arrangements perhaps and God knows what else.

Frank And if this guy was once a doctor or surgeon, he could maybe get medical files, or at least has a contact who can. But he can't work alone. Do you think Watson's partners involved ... whatsername?

Jenny Miss Peterson. Oh, God, Frank, there's still another one in the kitchen.

Frank What? You mean there's another one in the house? For Christ's sake, Jen, why didn't you ——

Jenny I locked it in.

Frank (*making for the cellar door*) Stay here. Don't come down, whatever you do.

Jenny Be careful, Frank.

The underscore begins again

Frank moves towards the cellar door, leaving Jenny. The underscore builds to a climax as Frank opens the door—to reveal that no-one is there

  Frank exits to the cellar kitchen. As he goes ...

Mr Watson jumps up, grabs Jenny and pulls the telephone wire round her throat. Jenny tries to scream out but merely chokes. Jenny reaches for the surgical case, grabs a pair of scissors from it and plunges them into Mr Watson's chest. He stands bolt upright for a moment, then slumps behind the sofa

Jenny crawls downstage, crying

Frank (*from the kitchen, off*) Jenny, Jenny, call the police now, quickly!

Jenny rushes to the phone and picks up the receiver; it is obvious that the line is dead

Jenny Oh, God, please — Frank, the line, it's dead! I think it's been cut ... Frank! Frank!

Frank runs in from the kitchen

Frank Jen, what is it?
Jenny Someone has cut the line. It's dead!
Frank That intruder has escaped through the skylight window. I'll go next door and see if I can use Jacqui's phone.
Jenny Don't leave me, Frank. I'm so frightened.
Frank Don't worry, Jen, I'll get the police. It won't be long before they catch her.
Jenny So you do think it's Peterson.
Frank It can't be anyone else. Watson would have to work closely with her to make sure he was covered whilst doubling up on his other roles.
Jenny I'm so glad it's over. I just can't stop shaking.

They hug each other tightly, Jenny crying quietly into Frank's arms

Frank It's over. She'll be on the run now. She won't get far, Jen. The police will soon catch up with her. The doors are all locked. We're safe. I promise.
Jenny I know, Frank. Just hold me for a second.

They embrace again. There is a moment's silence

Jacqui, still unrecognizable in her disguise, crashes through the stained glass window, a knife in her hand. This entrance is accompanied by appropriate sound effects and a dramatic burst of underscore music

Jacqui stabs Frank in the back; he falls to the floor with a yell of agony. Jenny turns and freezes at the threatening sight of the knife

The underscore holds a continuous tense chord. Jacqui circles round the horrified Jenny. At last, Jacqui pulls off her mask and screams in anger, controlled but terrifying

Jacqui You bastards, you've destroyed everything. You think you've been so clever.
Jenny Jacqui ...

Jacqui circles over to the cellar door, slams it shut and locks it

Jacqui Jacqui Henderson, Miss Peterson, call me what you like. You're dead. From the first day I met you my instinct told me we were going to have trouble with you two. I was right! Five years' work ruined because of you. I take it Harvey is dead?
Jenny Yes. But why, Jacqui, or whoever you are, why have you done all these terrible things?
Jacqui Why? Oh, that's simple: money, money, and greed and injustice. You see, when Dr Harvey was thrown out of his surgeon's practice by the Medical Association I was his nurse. Dr Harvey was a good man. He tried to help someone who was dying. They needed a kidney transplant. Then one day a young man was brought into the casualty department. He was dead — killed himself on a motorbike, the idiot. Dr Harvey was on duty that day and after exploratory surgery found out that this man's kidney was a perfect match. But then the doctor had a problem: the parents wouldn't give their permission for the operation. A young man who had spent his teens tearing around on a motorbike doing sod all; and now, for the first time in his miserable life, he had a chance of doing something — and his parents said no.
Jenny So what happened?

During the next speech, Frank crawls quietly to Mr Watson's case and picks up the revolver

Jacqui He did the operation anyway. We thought the parents would be none the wiser but they did find out, somehow, and Dr Harvey was arrested. He was struck off the medical register and spent two years in jail; it nearly killed him. It was while he was in jail he met someone from the Middle East in there for drug smuggling. They shared a cell together. During that time he heard how difficult it was for the Middle East to get vital organs for transplants and how the oil-rich Arabs would pay vast amounts to obtain them. I think it was then he first started to plan. On his release he told me how we could both get rich. There was only one problem — we needed a live body — but we soon got round that, right here in this little churchyard. You would have been number thirteen, unlucky for some. Now, however, you'll just be a body. It's a shame, really. To think of all that waste. But, you see, you've killed Dr Harvey. Now I'm going to kill you. (*She thrusts the knife towards Jenny*)

Jenny (*screaming*) Frank!

Jacqui I wouldn't bother screaming. Only the dead can hear you from here — and you're about to join them! (*She lunges towards Jenny again*)

Frank shoots Jacqui three times as——

——the CURTAIN *falls*

FURNITURE AND PROPERTY LIST

ACT I

SCENE 1

On stage: BEDROOM
        Double bed
        Bedside table
        Dressing table

        LIVING-ROOM
        Fire irons
        Drinks cabinet. *In it*: glasses
        Sofa. *On it*: cushions
        Coffee table. *On it*: magazines and newspapers, paper, pens
        Side table. *On it*: practical lamp and phone
        Clothes
        Books

Personal: **Miss Peterson**: bag. *In it*: packet of cigarettes, lighter

SCENE 2

Strike: Clothes
          Books

Set: Torch (*under coffee table*)

Off stage: Suitcases (**Frank**)
          Duty-free bag. *In it*: whisky (**Frank**)
          Torch (**Miss Peterson**)
          Overcoat (**Mr Watson**)
          Briefcase. *In it*: papers (**Mr Watson**)
          Coat (**Miss Peterson**)
          Bag (**Miss Peterson**)
          Jug of water (**Jenny**)

SCENE 3

Strike: Suitcases
              Duty-free bag
              Jug of water

Set: BEDROOM
              On dressing table: hairbrush, hairspray
              LIVING-ROOM
              Bottle of brandy

Re-set: Torch (*under table*)

Off stage: Bottle of champagne wrapped in paper (**Frank**)
              Golf umbrella (**Frank**)
              Blood-stained ice cooler box (**Mr Watson**)
              Plate of cheese sandwiches (**Jenny**)

ACT II

SCENE 1

Strike: Golf umbrella

Set: Two cups of coffee

Off stage: Two plastic bags. *In them*: shopping (**Frank**)
              Toolkit. *In it*: screwdriver (**Frank**)
              Two cups of coffee (**Jenny**)
              Tray of sandwiches (**Jenny**)
              Logs (**Frank**)
              Bloodstained spade (**Jenny**)

Personal: **Mr Harvey**: large handkerchief

SCENE 2

Strike: Spade
              Toolkit

Set: Bedroom
            Extension telephone
            Living Room
              In chimney: Laundry bag. *In it:* man's trousers, shirt, jacket,
              jumper, socks, Visa receipt, envelope. *In it:* medical papers

Off stage: Coat (**Frank**)
             Stick (**Frank**)
             Damp towel (**Frank**)

Scene 3

Strike: Laundry bag and contents

Set: Matches

Off stage: Two mugs of tea (**Jenny**)
             Jeans and jumper, shoes (**Frank**)
             Leather bag. *In it:* surgical instruments, including scissors and
               knives, revolver (**Mr Watson**)
             Knife (**Jacqui**)

Personal: **Mr Watson:** key

LIGHTING PLOT

Practical fittings required: lamp

1 interior with exterior backing

ACT 1, Scene 1. Late afternoon

To open: Darkness

Cue 1   *After* Curtain *rises*   (Page 1)
           Bring up general interior lighting; glow on stained
           glass window; sinking sun effect beyond windows
           throughout scene

Cue 2   **Mr Harvey:** "— till death us do part!"   (Page 7)
           Black-out

ACT 1, Scene 2. Late afternoon

To open: Exterior lighting fades to darkness throughout scene

Cue 3   **Frank** switches on lights   (Page 8)
           Snap on living-room lights

Cue 4   They kiss passionately   (Page 8)
           Fade exterior lights more quickly

Cue 5   **Jenny** switches on upstairs lights etc.   (Page 9)
           (See stage directions)
           Snap on lights upstairs, snap off lights downstairs;
           then reverse

Cue 6   **Frank** and **Jenny** embrace on the bed.   (Page 12)
           When ready
           Flash of lightning. Lights go out, leaving the
           stage in semi-darkness

Cue 7   **Frank:** "...the fuse box?"   (Page 12)
           Lights flicker back on

Cue 8	**Jenny** switches on more lights *Snap up more lights on living room*	(Page 17)
Cue 9	**Jenny** hangs up the phone *The Lights flicker and go out, then immediately come back on*	(Page 17)
Cue 10	**Jenny** moves to close the curtains *All lights go out in the chapel*	(Page 18)
Cue 11	**Jenny** shines the torch into the cellar *Flash of lightning*	(Page 18)
Cue 12	**Jenny** screams loudly *Black-out*	(Page 19)

ACT I, Scene 3. Late afternoon

To open: General interior lighting; darkness outside

Cue 13	**Jenny** switches on the light at the side table *Snap up practical lamp with covering spot*	(Page 26)

ACT II, Scene 1. Morning

To open: Bright general interior and exterior lighting

No cues

ACT II, Scene 2. Late afternoon

To open: General interior and exterior lights

No cues

ACT II, Scene 3. Night

To open: General interior lighting; darkness outside

Cue 14   **Jenny** switches off downstairs lights   (Page 49)
          Snap off downstairs lights

Cue 15   **Jenny** attempts to light the fire   (Page 50)
          Dim glow on fire

Cue 16   **Mr Watson** switches on cupboard light   (Page 50)
          Snap on cupboard light

EFFECTS PLOT

The underscore for this play is available on hire from MICHAEL ROSE LTD,
34, Glenville Road, Walkford, Christchurch, Dorset, BH23 5PY

ACT I

Cue 12   **Mr Watson** takes papers from his briefcase   (Page 15)
            Musical underscore begins

Cue 13   **Mr Watson:** "Why did they have to get here   (Page 16)
              early?"
            Distant roll of thunder; underscore stops

Cue 14   **Jenny** switches on more lights   (Page 17)
            The phone rings

Cue 15   **Jacqui Henderson** appears outside   (Page 18)
            Underscore begins

Cue 16   **Jenny** shines the torch into the cellar   (Page 19)
            Rumble of thunder

Cue 17   **Jenny** screams loudly   (Page 19)
            Underscore plays; fade when ready

Cue 18   **Mr Watson** emerges from behind the curtain   (Page 26)
            Underscore begins

Cue 19   **Mr Watson** passes the sofa   (Page 26)
            Phone rings

Cue 20   **Frank** turns to face the cellar door   (Page 27)
            Underscore begins to get faster and more menacing

ACT II

Cue 21   **Jenny** picks up the cups   (Page 29)
            Sound of a car pulling up

Cue 22   **Frank** tries to unscrew the door handle   (Page 32)
            Underscore begins

Cue 23   **Mr Harvey** moves towards **Frank**   (Page 32)
            Underscore builds in intensity

Cue 24   **Mr Harvey** closes in on **Frank**   (Page 33)
          Fade underscore

Cue 25   **Frank** tries to light the fire   (Page 35)
          Smoke

Cue 26   **Jenny:** "It's blood, fresh blood!"   (Page 36)
          Music; fade when ready

Cue 27   As Scene 2 begins   (Page 37)
          Phone rings

Cue 28   **Frank** goes back into the chimney   (Page 43)
          Underscore begins

Cue 29   Laundry bag falls on **Frank**   (Page 43)
          Underscore stops

Cue 30   **Frank:** "That's if we believe him."   (Page 45)
          Phone rings; underscore starts

Cue 31   **Jenny:** "Hallo. Who is there?"   (Page 46)
          Underscore stops

Cue 32   **Jacqui:** "... it's got to happen tonight."   (Page 48)
          Music

Cue 33   **Jenny** attempts to light the fire   (Page 50)
          Smoke

Cue 34   **Jenny** exits into the bathroom   (Page 50)
          Underscore begins

Cue 35   **Jenny** brushes her hair   (Page 50)
          Phone rings; fade underscore

Cue 37   **Mr Watson** hides under the stairs   (Page 51)
          Underscore begins

Printed in Great Britain by Redwood Books Limited, Trowbridge, Wiltshire